Aussie Slang Pictorial

Brolga Publishing Pty Ltd
PO Box 12544 A'Beckett St Melbourne Australia 8006
ABN 46 063 962 443
email: sales@brolgapublishing.com.au
web: www.brolgapublishing.com.au
e-mail: markzocchi@brolgapublishing.com.au

National Library of Australia Cataloguing-in-Publication entry

    Howey, Andrew.
    Aussie slang pictorial : what's it like mate / Andrew Howey.
    9781922175724 (pbk.)
    English language—Australia—Slang—Humor.
    English language—Australia—Slang—Humor—Pictorial works.
    427.994

Printed in China

Aussie Slang Pictorial

What's it like mate

Andrew Howey

A Lot

Too many irons in the fire
To have too many things, activities.

Too many fingers in the pie
Too many people interfering.

Too many cooks spoil the broth
Too many people in charge.

Too many chiefs and not enough Indians
Too many people in charge.

More of them than you can poke a stick at
A lot of items/things.

Heads on them like mice
A lot of them.

You must be the world's only living brain donor
Dumb or stupid to the extreme.

Too many fingers in the pie

All alone like a country dunny

Alone

Stands out like a bottle of milk
An expression of loneliness and isolation. Refers to the days when bottled milk was delivered to your door.

Let sleeping dogs lie
Leave well enough alone.

He shot through and left me sitting like a shag on a rock
Being left all alone.

Like a bandicoot on a burnt ridge
A state of loneliness and deprivation.

All dressed up with nowhere to go
Lonely, no friends, being stood up, or to have gone to an event at the wrong time.

All alone like a country dunny
Out in the middle of nowhere.

Two men and a dog
Often said of a place where there are not many people or very few people.

Drink with the flies
To drink alone.

Anger

Don't get your tits in a tangle
No need to get so angry.

Madder than a Baptist in a brothel
Really angry.

You got the "Jimmy Brits" (ie. Shits – state of anger)
Strine (Australian slang) for 'the shits'.

I'm so mad I'm going to hit you then stick you on a hot barbeque
Very angry.

Shit on the liver
In a foul mood.

Like a red rag to a bull
Anything that excites or induces anger.

Like a bear with a sore head
Bad-tempered, grumpy.

Don't get your knickers in a knot
No need to get so angry.

Come down like a ton of bricks
Scold someone severely.

Muck on the pluck
In a foul mood.

Don't get your knickers in a knot

You've got butterflies in your stomach

Anxious

More movement than a Swiss watch
Very nervous or active.

As toey as a Roman sandal
Extremely anxious; keen to start; excitable.

You're grasping at straws there
Getting desperate.

As nervous as a long-tailed cat in a room full of rocking chairs
Very nervous, anxious.

Butterflies in your stomach
To be extremely nervous.

Like a cat on a hot stove/tin roof
Extremely agitated, worried, nervous, jittery.

On pins and needles
Anxious; fretting; in an agitated or worried state.

Like a fart in a bottle
Agitated; unable to remain still.

As nervous as a mother 'roo in a room full of pickpockets
Very nervous.

Both Sides

On both sides of the fence
Having no loyalty to one side or the other.

You can't have one foot either side of the fence if it's made of barbed wire
You will make an error if you don't take one side or the other.

Bread is buttered on both sides
Having the best of both ways.

Can't run with the hare and hunt with the hounds
Cannot have it both ways.

You can't have one foot either side of the fence
if it's made of barbed wire

As busy as a blow-fly at a barbeque

Busy

As busy as a one-armed bill poster in a gale
As busy as a one legged bloke in an arse kicking contest
A sarcastic comment, that means you are not busy at all.

As busy as a one-armed paper hanger
As busy as a blow-fly at a barbeque
To be very busy or hyperactive.

As busy as a brickie in Beirut
As busy as a one-armed taxi driver with the crabs
As busy as a centipede on a hot plate
Very busy.

He couldn't find his arse with both hands, even if his fingers
were flashlights!
Real busy, or real stupid.

As busy as a one-eyed cat watching two rat holes
As busy as a one-armed milker on a dairy farm
Extremely busy.

Car

Handles like a bag of shit tied with a piece of string in the middle
A car that handles poorly.

Let's hit the "Frog 'n' toad" (ie. the road)
Strine expression for, let's hit the road.

It's got more herbs than a tractor
Acceleration of a car (more power).

Where did you get your license from, a Cornflakes Box?
A remark said to an incompetent driver.

Able to turn on a threepence
For a car with a very tight turning circle.

Only drove it to Church on a Sunday
Said of a car that's used very little.

If I didn't hit the anchors he'd be a goner
If I hadn't hit the brakes, he would have been in an accident.

It handles like a dog on lino
The car is all over the place.

Couldn't drive ducks to water
A hopeless car driver.

Couldn't drive a greasy stick up a dog's arse
Is a lousy driver.

Where did you get your licence from, a cornflakes box?

It's the squeaky wheel that gets the oil

Complain

Piss in it or get off the pot
Do something constructive instead of complaining about it.

It's the squeaky wheel that gets the oil
If you don't complain nobody will know.

Stop dragging the chain
You're not pulling your weight.

Squeal like a pig
Complain loudly.

What do you think this is, Bush Week?
A protest or complaint.

If you tripped over a gold bar, you'd complain about your toe
A person who whinges or complains.

Cop it sweet
Don't complain.

Compliment

Your blood's worth bottling
Said to someone who is admired, or has done something excellent.

A better man never stood in two shoes
You are a fine man.

You're true blue
You are a good person.

Take to something like a duck to water
Adapt well to new circumstances.

You know your chalk from cheese
You can easily recognise what is the right thing to do.

Your blood's worth bottling

He's got tickets on himself

Conceited

Head was so far up his arse if he farted he would whistle
Has a very high opinion of himself.

Too big for your boots
You're vain.

He thinks he's hot shit, but he's only a cold fart warmed up
Has a high opinion of himself.

Thinks the sun shines out of his arse
To have a high opinion of oneself.

Thinks he's the ant's pants/the cat's whiskers/the bee's knees
An inflated ego.

He thinks he's the cat's pyjamas
Thinks he is better than next person.

He's got tickets on himself
Highly self-opinionated person.

A legend in one's own mind
Conceited person.

Let the devil take the hindmost
A selfish statement that those following, will have to look after themselves.

Blow your own trumpet
Boast, brag about yourself.

Dislike

Drag his name through the mud
Speak ill of someone.

I wouldn't piss on him if he was on fire
Said of someone who is disliked.

Wouldn't be seen dead with you in a forty-acre paddock
Is not held in high regard.

May your chooks turn into emus and kick your dunny down
I dislike you.

Pull your lip over your head and swallow
An insult of sorts.

If brains were dynamite, he wouldn't have enough to blow his nose
An insult to someone lacking intelligence.

May the fleas of a thousand camels infest your armpits
You're basically scum.

You're a waste of space
I don't think too highly of you.

Drag his name through the mud

This'll put hairs on his chest

Drinking

Under the affluence of incahol
Simply drunk.

I'll be twitching like a burning corpse
Often said after having too much coffee.

Didn't touch the sides
Referring to a drink that was insufficient for one's thirst.

Guaranteed to kill a germ at twenty paces
A very strong or potent drink, with alcohol in it.

A two pot screamer
Very susceptible to alcohol. This person gets drunk easily.

I'm so thirsty, I'd drink it out of an old sock
Very thirsty.

Mouth tastes like a monkey's armpit
To experience an unpleasant taste (usually after a night of consuming alcoholic drinks).

This'll put hairs on your chest
When you drink this you'll be a man.

Wouldn't shout in a shark attack
Will not take his/her turn buying the drinks in a bar.

You can't walk on one leg
An expression said after being offered a drink, after you have finished your first drink.

Fuller than a seaside dunny on Boxing Day
Intoxicated (Boxing Day—hot!)

Had a skinful
Inebriated or fed up with someone.

A man's not a camel
I'm thirsty.

Hair of the dog
Having an alcoholic drink the morning after to cure a hangover.

I'm so thirsty I could drink the sweat from a Japanese Sumo wrestler's jockstrap
Very thirsty.

He'd drink the piss out of a brewer's horse
He's an alcoholic.

In the grip of the grape
A wino or an alcoholic.

Mouth feels like the bottom of a bird's cage
To experience an unpleasant taste (usually after a night of consuming alcoholic drinks).

I'll have a ten ounce sandwich
A lunch consisting only of beer.

As drunk as Chloe
Very Drunk. Refers to the Melbourne hotel, Young and Jackson, and the painting of Chloe.

I'm so thirsty I could drink it out of an old sock

He's got a few roos loose in the top paddock

Dumb

Wouldn't know if a band were up him until they hit the drum
His elevator doesn't go to the top floor
A few bites short of a biscuit
Hasn't got enough brains to get a headache
If you had another brain it would be lonely
Couldn't go two rounds with a revolving door
A couple of tinnies short of a slab
Someone who is simple minded.

As sharp as a bowling ball
Someone who is lacking in intelligence. Bowling balls aren't sharp at all.

A few shelves short of a cabinet
He's got a few roos loose in the top paddock
Doesn't have it together.

A couple of sandwiches short of a picnic
Dumb.

One brick short of a load
Mentally challenged.

A sausage short of the barbecue
Short of brains (a snag short of a barbie).

Dumber than a wagon-load of rocks
Not troubled by intelligence.

Easy

Like a greasy stick up a dead-dog's arse
Easily with no effort.

Like shooting fish in a barrel
An extremely easy task.

As easy as pie
Very easy.

As easy as spearing an eel with a spoon
Not easy at all.

As easy as putting butter up an echidna's bum with a knitting needle on a hot summer's day
A sarcastic way of saying not easy.

Like taking candy from a baby
An extremely easy task.

Do it with one arm tied behind my back
Doing something with great ease.

As easy as falling off a log
Very easy.

Like taking candy from a baby

Born with a silver spoon in one's mouth

Family

Trouble and strife and billy lids
Strine for the wife and kids.

He got the rounds of the kitchen from the "trouble 'n' strife"
Strine expression for wife.

Go home to the ball and chain
The wife.

The black sheep (of the family)
An outcast or disreputable member of the family.

Born with a silver spoon in one's mouth
From a wealthy family.

Born with a wooden spoon in one's mouth
From a poor family.

Born on the wrong side of the tracks
From the poor side of town.

Keep up with the Jones'
Pertaining to the competition between neighbours over material possessions.

Wet the baby's head
Celebrate the baby's birth.

Fight

I'll give you Bondi
Give you a beating. Bondi is a Sydney suburb.

I'll pin your ears back (if you're not careful)
I'll knock your teeth so far down your throat, that you'll have
to stick your toothbrush up your arse to clean them
A threat of violence.

Rafferty's rules
No rules at all.

Knuckle Sandwich
A punch in the mouth.

It was on for young and old
An outbreak of disorder.

Dog and Goanna rules
No rules, whatsoever.

Give 'em heaps
To contest strongly.

I'll beat you like a redheaded stepchild
The child's hair was blonde, however, it is now red after all the beatings.

She's open slather
Where the forces of law and order turn a blind eye.

I will give you a knuckle sandwich

As full as a butcher's dog

Food

Could eat a baby's bum through a cane chair
Could eat a galah and bark sandwich
Could eat a goanna between two slabs of bark
Very hungry.

A snag's not a snag without a bit of "dead horse" (ie. tomato sauce)
Strine for tomato sauce.

Full as a fat lady's knickers
Full of food.

Have the run of your dover
Eat all you want.

Could eat the crotch out of a low flying duck
Very hungry.

Could crack a flea on yer' stomach
Suggesting you've eaten too much.

As full as a butcher's dog
Full of food.

My stomach thinks my throat has been cut
I'm hungry.

Fun

Lay them in the aisles
Be extremely funny.

Burn the candle at both ends
Living a strenuous life, active day and night, partying hard.

The night's a pup
It's early yet.

Last one in is a rotten egg
A jocular expression, enticing a group to jump into a pool.

Burn the midnight oil
Staying up very late.

The most fun you can have with your pants on
Now, that's a lot of fun.

Having a whale of a time
Having a really enjoyable time.

Haven't had this much fun since Granny got her tits
A jocular expression of pleasure.

Paint the town red
Have a celebration, go out on the town.

You are a stick in the mud
You're not much fun, not adventurous.

As much fun as beer, women and skittles
Now that's fun.

Burn the candle at both ends

He'd bet on two flys walking up the wall

Gamble

It ran like a hairy goat
The racehorse didn't run well.

He'd bet on two flies walking up the wall
A compulsive gambler.

He's got more tips than an asparagus field
Someone who thinks he has all the inside knowledge, but invariably doesn't.

The dogs are barking for this one
A horse which is a hot tip will have the dogs barking.

Here's a bit of braille for you
Here's a tip.

And you can bet London to a brick on that, he'll chicken out!
Bet London to win a brick, made famous by race caller Ken Howard.

Come in spinner
Here's another sucker.

I'll eat the horse and chase the jockey
Expression from a disappointed punter.

A roll Jack Rice couldn't jump over
Jack Rice was a champion hurdler.

Good

Life is a bed of roses
Quality of life is good.

To make one's marble good
To improve.

Best thing this side of the Black Stump
The 'Black Stump' is the imaginary last post of civilisation.

Better than a poke in the eye with a burnt stick
Things could be worse.

Best thing since sliced bread
Simply, it's the best thing.

Everything is apples
Everything is okay.

Bright-eyed and bushy-tailed
A person who is in good health and spirits and ready to go.

Dig a hole and bury me, it just doesn't get better than this!
This is the best thing.

Better than a slap in the face with a wet fish
Things could be far worse.

You are true blue
You are a good person.

You're true blue

As innocent as a cat in a goldfish bowl

Guilt

Laura Norda
Strine for law and order.

Like a piano player in a brothel
Someone implicated but no moral responsibility.

As innocent as a cat in a goldfish bowl
A sarcastic statement indicating one is guilty. Not innocent at all.

Come up smelling of roses
To be found innocent after some wrong doing.
Caught with one's pants down
Caught doing something incriminating.
Suddenly you are disadvantaged.

Happy

Smiling like a Cheshire cat
Extremely pleased with yourself.

As happy as a box of birds
As happy as Larry
As happy as a dog with two tails
As happy as a dog in a hubcap factory
As happy as a worm in a can on the way home from a fishing trip
As happy as a possum up a gumtree
As happy as a pig in mud
Supremely happy; in high spirits.

Smiling from one ear to the other
Extremely pleased with yourself.

You look like the cat that swallowed the canary/cream/mouse
Said of someone who looks pleased with themselves.

As happy as a pig in mud

You could eat dinner off the floor

Home

I'm a stone's throw away
I'm very close to home or where you are.

I'm on the "Pat Malone" (ie. You're home alone)
Strine for 'I am home alone'.

It's triple-fronted brick vanilla
Ironic term for the typical suburban dream home.

Pull up stumps
Moving home, changing address.

He's on the dog and bone
Strine for being on the telephone.

I'm up the apple and pears
Strine for being up the stairs.

Back to the Cactus
Return to the home or familiar haunts.

You could eat your dinner off the floor
The house is very clean.

Keep the home fires burning
Maintain a welcoming environment at home.

Impossible

That'll be the day
It will never happen.

A leopard cannot change its spots
Said of a person (usually bad), that they cannot change their ways.

Can't get blood out of stone
Cannot extract something from something that doesn't have it.

Not for all the tea in China
No, under no circumstances.

You've got two chances, none and Buckley's
You got no chance.

Can't put a square peg in a round hole
It cannot be done.

It's like pushing shit up hill with a pointy stick
Attempting the impossible.

Buckley's chance
Impossible.

I can't for the life of me
Under no circumstances.

Can't get blood out of a stone

He lets the grass grow under his feet

Lazy

He wouldn't work in an iron lung
Very lazy.

He's like London fog. That bludger never lifts
This person never does any work.

Don't bust your boiler
Don't try too hard.

Don't stand around like a bottle of stale piss
Don't be forlorn or idle, start doing something.

He couldn't get a job as a road hump
Slow witted, lethargic.

As lively as a blowie on a winter's day
A lethargic person.

He lets the grass grow under his feet
He has become idle, lazy.

Leave

If I wanted to talk to an asshole like you, I would've farted
Go away and leave me alone.

You are as welcome as a fart in a phone box
Get out of here.

Make like a shepherd and get the flock out of here
Got to get outta here!

Vote with one's foot
To express one's disapproval by leaving, or a demonstration.

He did like a horse's dick and hit the road
He left!

Off like a bucket of prawns in the hot sun
Leaving quickly.

Going to make like a baby.
Head out, leave.

Shoot through like a Bondi tram
To depart in haste. Bondi being a suburb in Sydney.

Make like a tree (and leave)
Leave.

I'm going to "Harold Holt" (ie. bolt)
Strine for bolt. Harold Holt was an Australian Prime Minister, who disappeared at sea.

Go to Billyo
Get lost.

As welcome as a fart in a phone booth

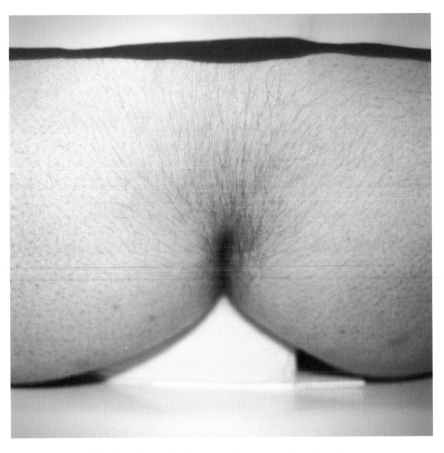

You've landed your bum in the butter

Lucky

Think all your Christmas's have come at once
To have good fortune.

You've landed with your bum in the butter
To experience good luck after misfortune.

Coming up smelling of roses
Got oneself out of trouble.

Laughing all the way to the bank
Experience good fortune.

Got more arse than class
Success achieved through chance rather than planning.

Mad

Got only one oar in the water
Mad.

You're one sick puppy
A depraved person. From an image of psychologically disturbed puppy.

Like a blue-arsed fly
In a frenzied manner.

Going off, like a frog in a sock.
Going crazy.

Off one's kadoova
Deranged, off one's head.

As mad as a meat axe
Mad as a cut snake
He's got nits in the network
Crazy, insane.

Mad as a gum tree full of galahs
Off one's pannikin
Off your head, pannikin (small metal drinking cup).

To have bats in the belfry
Crazy, insane.

As nutty as a fruit cake
Foolish, eccentric.

Mad as a meat axe

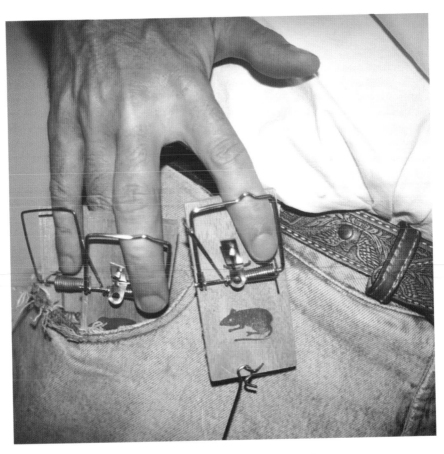

Has mouse traps in his pockets

Mean

He wouldn't give you a light for your pipe at a bushfire
Wouldn't give you a wave if he owned the ocean
Wouldn't give you a fright if he was a ghost
Wouldn't give you a shock if he owned the powerhouse
Wouldn't give a dog a drink at his mirage
So tight you couldn't drive a pin up his arse with a sledgehammer
Someone who is miserly.

So mean, he would steal the gold fillings out of his grandmother's grave
You're the sort that licks the bowl when they have finished, rather than
pull the chain
Penny-pinching with money.

Wouldn't give you his sleeves out of his vest
Said of a person mean with money.

Short arms long pockets
Still has his lunch money from school
Someone who will not part with his money.

Has mouse traps in his pockets
No wonder he never puts his hand in his pocket to pay for anything/give anyone a hand.

So mean that when a fly lands in the sugar he shakes its feet before he
kills it
Mean as they come.

Mistake

No use shutting the door after the horse has bolted
It's too late to do, after an error.

Throw a spanner in the works!
Screw it up, or to make an error.

Don't count your chickens before they are hatched
A warning not to anticipate the outcome, for it may turn out different than you expected.

Throw a fly in the ointment!
To make an error or screw something up.

You don't throw the baby out with the bath water
Don't throw out everything, let's only remove what's bad.

Pull out mate, the dogs are pissing on your swag
Advice to abandon the track you are on.

Don't put all your eggs in one basket
Don't risk everything on the one enterprise.

In like a lion, out like a lamb
To be deflated after the failure of a boastful act.

Barking up the wrong tree
Pursuing the wrong purpose.

The straw that broke the camel's back
The final incident that leads to mishap.

Throw a fly in the ointment

So poor he is licking paint off the fence

Money

Champagne taste on a beer income
Living, or desiring to live, beyond your means.

Anyone would think money grew on trees
There's not enough money and it's being spent too freely.

Burn a hole in one's pocket
Pertaining to great expense.

Cost an arm and a leg
Expensive.

Whale in the bay
A person with money to spend.

As poor as a church mouse/bandicoot
Very poor.

Haven't got a cracker (or a brass razoo)
Got no money. Razoo is a fictitious coin.

Charge like the light brigade
An expensive fee. Referring to the light brigade during World War I.

Live off the smell of a oily rag
Metaphor for ability to be able to survive on little.

So poor he is licking paint off the fence
Very poor

Charge like wounded bulls
Charge high prices.

Obvious

Can't see the grass for the trees
Lacking insight.

Do bears shit in the woods?
Yes! Obviously!

Stands out like a black crow in a bucket of milk
Obvious, extremely clear.

Does the Pope tuck his shirt in with a wooden spoon
Of course he does. YES!

Does Raggedy Anne have cotton tits
Of course she does.

Does a Koala shit in a gum tree and wipe his ass on a Cockatoo?
Most likely.

Sticks out like dogs balls
Very clear, self-evident.

Is the Pope Catholic?
Yes! Obviously!

Can't see the trees for the forest
Lacking insight

Even blind Freddy could see that
Blatantly obvious (blind Freddy a fictitious person representing the lowest level of perception and competence).

Stands out like a crow in a bucket of milk

It stood out like a lily in a dustbin

Out of Place

Like a fish out of water
Uncomfortable in unfamiliar surroundings.

Stand out like a sore finger/toe
To be prominent, conspicuous.

Like a spare groom at a wedding
Out of place, not needed.

Like a pick-pocket at a nudist camp
Out of place, not comfortable with the surroundings.

He was as out of place as a beer bottle in the Colosseum
Incongruous. There are/were no beer bottles in the Colosseum

A grape on the business
The odd man out.

It stood out like a lily on a dustbin
Conspicuous.

Stand out like tits on a bull
To be prominent, conspicuous.

Rest

Have a camp
In need of a rest.

Dead on one's feet
Exhausted.

Put one's cue in the rack
Have a rest.

I'm going for a kip
Have a nap.

A cup of tea, a Bex, and a good lie down
A stock phrase to describe a once popular method of relaxation. Often an expression, said between two females. Bex is an Australian product used as a relaxant.

Dead to the world
Asleep.

Check one's eyelids for holes
Having a sleep.

Couldn't raise a gallop
Physically exhausted.

Hit the hay
Go to bed.

Hit the hay

Between you, me and a gate post

Secret

Sweep it under the carpet
To conceal or cover up a problem or incident.

Between you, me and the gate post
Confidential.

Let the cat out of the bag
Reveal a secret.

Play your cards close to your chest
Be secretive.

The right hand must never know what the left is doing
Pertaining to complete secrecy.

A shut mouth catches no flies
A warning not to reveal any secrets or confidences.

It's alright, I won't talk outta school
I can keep a secret.

Sex

Turn the lights out and play hide the sausage
Jocular expression for sexual play or intercourse.

It's like a flock of sparrows flyin' out of yer arse
An expression for the male orgasm.

Randier than a stud bull let lose in a paddock full of heifers
Very randy.

So hard a dog wouldn't sink a tooth in it
Pertaining to an erection of the penis.

You could hang your wet duffel coat on those
She's got prominent nipples.

Why go out for a hamburger when you have steak at home
A sexual compliment to your live in partner.

You don't have to look at the mantelpiece when stoking the fire
Said of someone who is a potential sexual partner, no matter how ugly.

He'd go the barber's floor if it had enough hair on it
A man who is indiscriminate with his sexual partners.

Awning over the toyshop
Awning equals beer gut and so toyshop is…

Stairway to heaven
A run or ladder in a woman's stockings.

They all said she had the sweetest "lemonade 'n' sars"
Strine for a good arse.

Just like a wombat — he eats, roots, shoots and leaves

He could squeeze my toothpaste

Walking around like a three-legged dog
A man with three legs, or two legs and a hard penis.

Lie back and think of England
Said by ladies when having sex with a man and not enjoying it.

It's like putting marshmallow into a money box
Trying to insert a less than erect penis into a vagina

Get the dirty water off your chest
Have sexual intercourse.

Like having a shower with a raincoat on
Used by men to describe wearing a condom.

Member of the Wandering Hands Society
A man who has his hand all over a woman.

Just like a wombat - he eats, roots, shoots and leaves
A female expression pertaining to the sexual nature of men.

Caught in a circular saw
Metaphor for female promiscuity.

Hawk the fork
To engage in prostitution.

She can park her shoes under my bed
Jocular description of one's desire for another.

You can bark but you're not allowed to bite
Referring to a male's obsession for viewing women.

He could squeeze my toothpaste
An attractive male.

Slow

He's further back than a snake's arse
He is a long way behind.

You turn like a corkscrew
You are real slow.

As exciting as watching grass grow
A sarcastic expression. Very slow or boring.

It's like watching paint dry
Very boring and slow.

Too slow to keep worms in a tin
Very slow.

As slow as a wet week
Very slow and/or boring.

He's about as a rapid as a glacier
Not quick at all.

Stop dragging the chain
You're not pulling your weight. You are either lazy or slow.

Drag the chain
To lag behind.

As slow as a month of Sundays
Very slow, boring or said of someone who is dumb.

As exciting as watching grass grow

Dangle a carrot under someone's nose

Talk

Would talk a glass eye to sleep
An excessive bore.

Yer talking farmyard confetti
A whole load of rubbish.

Mouth like a horse's collar
A big mouth.

Couldn't talk if one lost one's arm
Said of someone who waves the hands and arms when speaking.

Save yer breath to cool the porridge
Stop talking so much.

Talk under wet cement with a mouthful of marbles
Usually a pub bore.

Boomerang Bender
Teller of tall stories.

Got too much of what the cat licks itself with
Too talkative.

Could eat an apple through a picket fence
A big mouth.

Talk the leg off a wooden table/chair
To talk too much.

Can talk under water
Loud talker.

Beating around the bush
Not getting to the point on a subject.

Talk so much, that in summer your tongue gets burnt
Someone who talks excessively.

Take the words out of my mouth
That's exactly what I was going to say.

She wouldn't say dick if her mouth was full of it!
Doesn't say much.

Last time I saw a mouth like that, it had a hook in it
Big mouth.

If bullshit was snow he'd be a blizzard
Talks nonsense.

If bullshit was music he'd be a concerto
Talks nonsense.

He could sell a boomerang to the Aborigines
Could sell anything.

He could talk a dog off a meat-wagon.
Someone who can be very persuasive.

Dangle a carrot under someone's nose
Tempt or bribe someone.

Like a fly on the wall
Eavesdropping on other's conversation.

Like a fly on the wall

Have one foot in the grave and the other on a banana peel

Trouble

Things are crook in Tallarook
Strine for things are crook. Tallarook is a town in Victoria.

My father will have my guts for garters
I'm in trouble.

Between a rock and a hard place
In a predicament, or vulnerable position.

Got one foot in the grave and the other on a banana peel
In a real predicament.

When the shit hits the fan
When the crisis becomes public.

Up the creek in a barbed wire canoe
In a dire predicament.

Stirring the possum
Deliberately causing trouble.

Set the cat amongst the pigeons
Create trouble, cause havoc.

More trouble than the early settlers
In a lot of trouble.

Out of the frying pan and into the fire
From one bad situation into something worse.

In more shit than a Werribee duck
Werribee being a place in Melbourne where the sewerage is stored.

Ugly

I've seen better heads on a boil
Ugly.

A face like a mouthful of mashed up Smarties
Ugly. Smarties are a chocolate sweet.

Hair like a birch broom in a fit
Your hair is a mess.

Fell out of the ugly tree and hit every branch on the way
Very ugly.

She could scare buzzards off of a meat wagon!
She's ugly.

A face like a festered pickle bottle. Yuck!
Looks like something the cat dragged in
Looking horrid.

Got a face like a mile of unpaved road
Pretty ugly.

I've seen better heads on a beer
An unpleasant countenance.

Got a face like a stopped clock
Ugly.

A face like a mouthful of smashed Smarties

As useless an an ashtray on a motorbike

Ugly

As ugly as a box of blowflies
Head like a beaten favourite
A face like a twisted sandshoe
Head like a half-eaten pasty
An ugly face.

As ugly as a bulldog chewing a wasp
Face like a burnt thong
As ugly as a bag of spanners
Ugly.

He's got a head on him like a Dirranbandi mailbag
Ugly. Dirranbandi is an outback town in Queensland.

Ugly as a deep sea racing mullet!
Ugly chick.

Face like a smashed crab
Ugly.

If I had a dog that looked like him, I'd shave its arse and make it
walk backwards
He had a head on him like a sucked mango
A face like a marron and hands like a couple of yabbies
Ugly.

You look like you have been chasing parked cars
Appear to have been beaten up, around the face.

Useless

As useless as an ashtray on a motorbike
As useless as tits on a bull
As useless as a glass door on a dunny
As useless as a hip pocket in a singlet
As useless as a chocolate teapot
As useless as a waterproof teabag
As useless as a bucket under a bull
As useless as mudflaps on a speedboat
As useless as a roo-bar on a skateboard
As useless as a sliding door on a submarine
Couldn't pour a drink out of a shoe if the instructions were
written on the heel
Couldn't organise anything.

Needed like a back pocket in a t-shirt
Not needed at all.

Couldn't give away cheese at a rats' picnic
Utterly hopeless.

It's raining cats and dogs

Beyond the back of Bourke

Weather

Wet enough to bog a duck
It has rained a lot.

Bourke shower
A dust storm. Bourke is an outback town in New South Wales.

It's raining cats 'n' dogs
Heavy storm or rain.

It was so wet even the mirages overflowed!
Very wet.

So windy it'd blow a blue dog off its chain
Very windy.

Acknowledgements

I would like to thank all those people who have so bravely surrendered their daily routines to help me in the production of the book's images, as models and assistants.

Sofia Carvounaris, Kerrie Vasiliadis, Chris Purificato, Ermanno Lughi, Justin Scavo, Vincent Ascone, Matthew Mizzi, Gianni Luczek, Adrian Saccio, Claude Di Vito, Sotirios Ioannidis, Amanda Iuele, Lisa Iuele, Connie Carter, Clint Padula, the dog Monthy and the Piggott family, Les and son Connor, Terry, Tony at La Porchetta in Mill Park, Dave at Goudge Automotive, and Adam.

A special thanks to those who let their properties available for some of the shots, you know who you are. Bryan from Mathoura NSW you might recognise your outdoor dunny in here, you should be bloody proud of her, she's gone a long way!

A very special thanks to my family, here and overseas, for their everlasting support and love.

Nik MacGregor of Red Vision Photography

Thank you to my wife, Jacqui, for her love and support with my endeavours. Not only for this book, but for the other mad-capped ideas I have. I would also like to thank my family, Anne, Stephen, Peter, Jean and Bob who have heard it from me, all before. Special thanks to Nik. Without him this book would not be possible.

Andrew Howey

Sanitaruim™ is a registered trademark Registered trademark of Australasian Conference Association Limited (ACAL)™ Trademark of ACAL Stock images provided by Wildlight and Australian Picture Library.

Andrew Howey and Nik MacGregor
"The short and tall of it"

ALSO AVAILABLE
FROM BROLGA PUBLISHING

Aussie Slang Dictionary
$17.99 • 9781921596155 • 180pp

The *Aussie Slang Dictionary* is here to help you decipher and speak the true local language. Full of dazzling definitions from true-blue Aussies, you'll never be lost for words with this collection of colourful sayings. From 'aerial ping-pong' (AFL) to 'on the wrong tram' (to be following the wrong train of thought) and finishing up with some verbal diarrhoea (never-ending blather), your mind will be brimming with useful (and not so useful!) sayings for your next run-in with a true Aussie character.

AUSSIE SLANG PICTORIAL

Qty

RRP AU$19.99 .....

Postage within Australia AU$5.00 .....

TOTAL★ $_____ ★All prices include GST

Name: ....Phone:...

Address: ....

Email: ....

Payment: ❏ Money Order ❏ Cheque ❏ MasterCard ❏ Visa

Cardholder's Name: ....

Credit Card Number: __ __ __ __   __ __ __ __   __ __ __ __   __ __ __ __

Signature: ....Expiry Date: __ __ / __ __

Allow 7 days for delivery.

Payment to: Marzocco Consultancy (ABN 14 067 257 390)
                PO Box 12544
                A'Beckett Street, Melbourne, 8006
                Victoria, Australia
                admin@brolgapublishing.com.au

BE PUBLISHED

Publish through a successful publisher.
Brolga Publishing is represented through:
• **National** book trade distribution, including sales,
marketing & distribution through **Macmillan Australia.**
• **International** book trade distribution to
   • The United Kingdom
   • North America
   • Sales representation in South East Asia
• **Worldwide e-Book distribution**

For details and inquiries, contact:
Brolga Publishing Pty Ltd
PO Box 12544
A'Beckett St VIC 8006

Phone: 0414 608 494
markzocchi@brolgapublishing.com.au
ABN: 46 063 962 443
(Email for a catalogue request)